The editors would like to thank
BARBARA KIEFER, Ph.D.,
Charlotte S. Huck Professor of Children's Literature,
The Ohio State University, and
SARAH MORGAN, National Examiner,
United States Pony Club,
for their assistance in the preparation of this book.

Visit us on the Web!
randomhouse.com/kids
Seussville.com

Educators and librarians, for a variety of teaching tools, visit us at
randomhouse.com/teachers

Library of Congress Cataloging-in-Publication Data
Worth, Bonnie.
If I ran the horse show : all about horses / by Bonnie Worth ; illustrated by Aristides Ruiz and
Joe Mathieu. — 1st ed.
  p. cm. — (The Cat in the Hat's learning library)
Includes bibliographical references and index.
ISBN 978-0-375-86683-8 (trade) — ISBN 978-0-375-96683-5 (lib. bdg.)
1. Horses—Juvenile literature. I. Ruiz, Aristides, ill. II. Mathieu, Joseph, ill. III. Title.
SF302.W67 2012   636.1—dc23   2011024236

Printed in the United States of America   10 9 8 7 6 5 4 3 2 1   First Edition

If I Ran the
Horse Show

by Bonnie Worth

illustrated by Aristides Ruiz and Joe Mathieu

The Cat in the Hat's Learning Library®

Random House 🏠 New York

I'm the Cat in the Hat!
And today we will go
to my Super-Tremendous
Stupendous Horse Show!

ut I warn you, I might

et a little bit sappy.

hen it comes to horses,

get really happy!

SUPER-
TREMENDOUS
STUPENDOUS
HORSE SHOW

Horses and people
have long worked as one.
They've formed a strong bond,
when all's said and done.

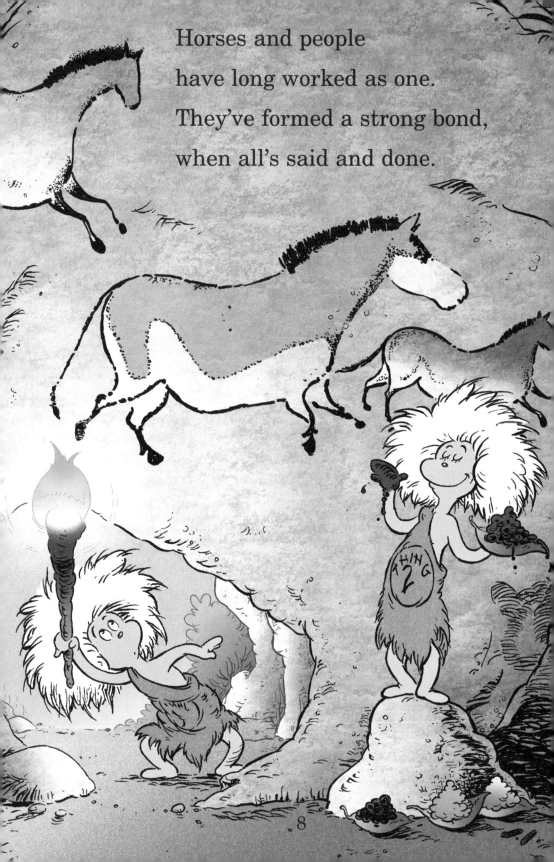

Horses were hunted
by cavemen as prey.

Farmers learned later
to make them obey.

All horses are treated
(you will find this fact fun)
as if they were born
on January one.

MARE/DAM

A foal is a horse who
is less than one year.
A yearling (surprise!)
is a year—is that clear?

FOAL

A filly's a female
who is less than four.
A mare is a female
who's four years or more.

colt is a male horse
ho is less than four.
stallion's a male
ho's four years or more.

dam is a horse
ho is also a mama.
sire is a stallion,
horse's papa.

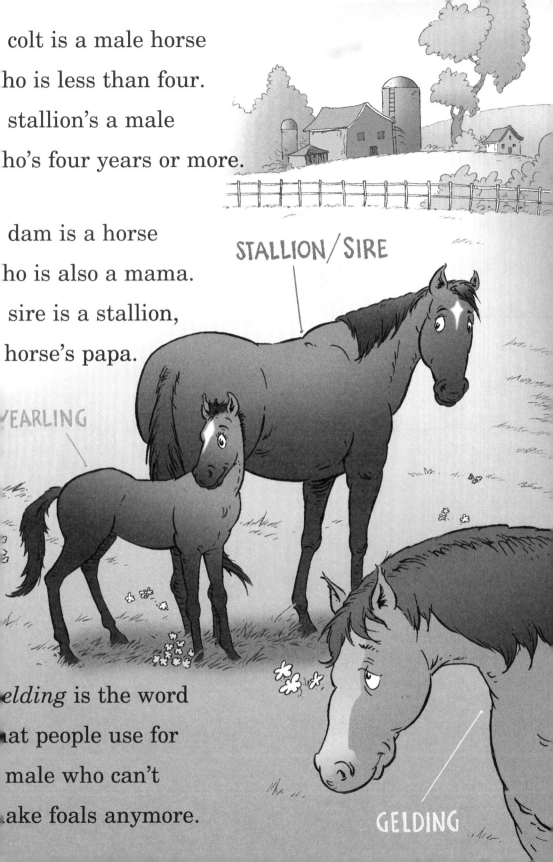

STALLION/SIRE

YEARLING

elding is the word
at people use for
male who can't
ake foals anymore.

GELDING

Before we go on,
it is good, I suppose,
to look at a horse
from its tail to its nose.

The top of the tail is
what we call the dock.
Then haunch and stifle
and gaskin and hock.
Hip, loins, back, flank,
withers, poll, crest.

Now take a deep breath
and go on with the rest.
Neck, jaw, and chin groove,
forehead and foretop,
nostril and muzzle—
is it time to stop?

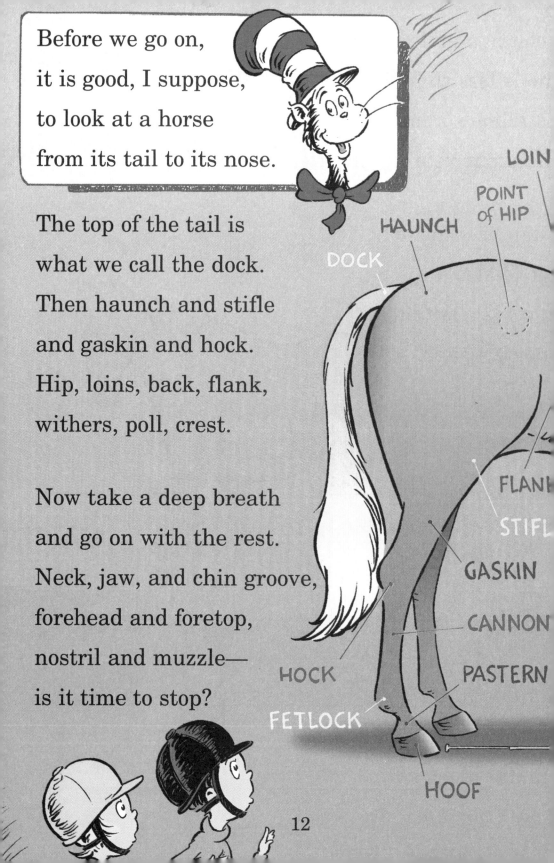

LOIN

POINT
of HIP

HAUNCH

DOCK

FLANK

STIFL

GASKIN

CANNON

PASTERN

HOCK

FETLOCK

HOOF

POLL

FORETOP

CREST

FOREHEAD

NECK

MUZZLE

NOSTRIL

WITHERS

BACK

JAW

CHIN GROOVE

POINT of SHOULDER

CHEST

FOREARM

ELBOW

KNEE

CORONET

No! Our look at the horse
can't be rated complete
until we have looked at
the legs and the feet.

Hoof, coronet, pastern,
knee and fetlock,
elbow and cannon,
then back to the hock!

Nerves under horsehide
can feel a fly creeping.
A tail fends off flies
by swatting and sweeping.

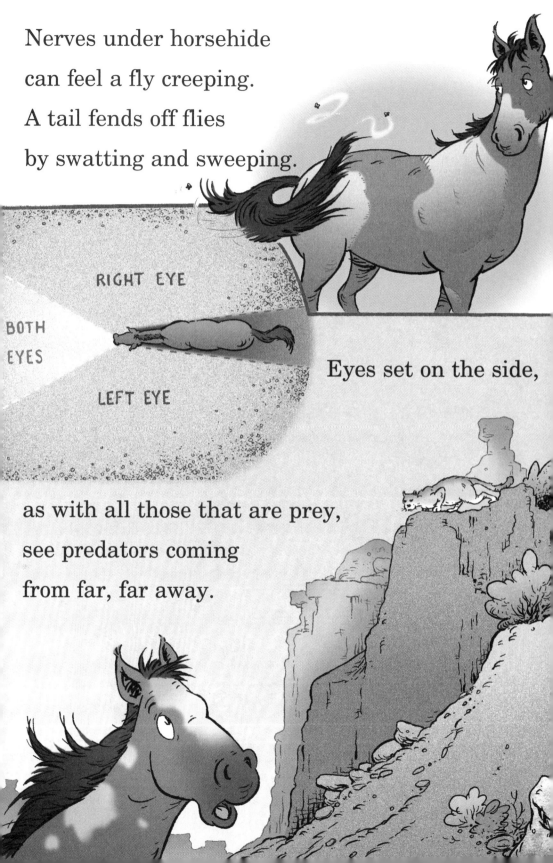

RIGHT EYE

BOTH
EYES

LEFT EYE

Eyes set on the side,

as with all those that are prey,
see predators coming
from far, far away.

Legs made for running
help horses to hie.
Flat hooves keep them steady
on wet turf or dry.

Most horses we ride—
this will not be big news—
have hooves that are guarded
by strong iron shoes.

Horse hooves, like your nails,
are made up of stuff
that doesn't have feeling.
Oh, hoof stuff is tough!

A farrier trims
horses' hooves with a file.
Horses should have this done
every once in a while.

16

He heats up horseshoes
until they are hot,
then nails them on tight.
Does it hurt? It does not!

Horses step out, or move,
at a number of rates.

Walk, trot,

canter, gallop—

we call these steps gaits.

Standardbred horses
can move at a pace,
a fast gait they use
when they run in a race.

The Icelandic pony
has what's called a tolt,
a swift gait that's smooth,
with nary a jolt.

Both Standard and Icy,
these two that you see,
are what we call breeds.
What are breeds? you ask me.

They are horses who mix
with similar mates
and give birth to foals
who have the same traits.

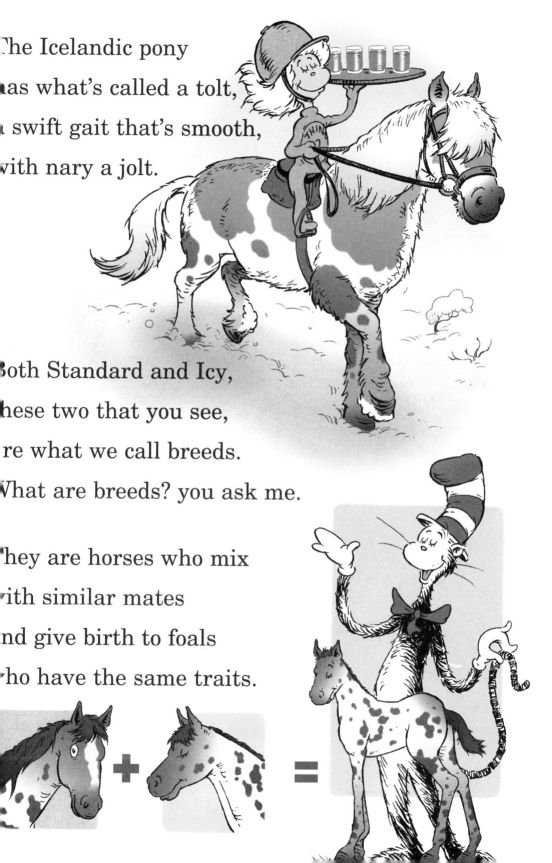

This breed is a Clydesdale.

It's bred to be big.

The Falabella is as small

as a six-month-old pig.

The Clydesdale, we know,
measures eighteen hands high.
The Falabella is seven.
What a cute little guy!

A hand is four inches.
It equals the span
of a hand that belongs
to a fully grown man.

We start from the ground
and then measure till we
get up to the withers—
no higher. You see?

Quarter horse is a breed
that started out West.
It's easy to handle and
herds cows the best.

Appaloosas are horses
that are covered with spots.
Native Americans liked
this spotted breed lots.

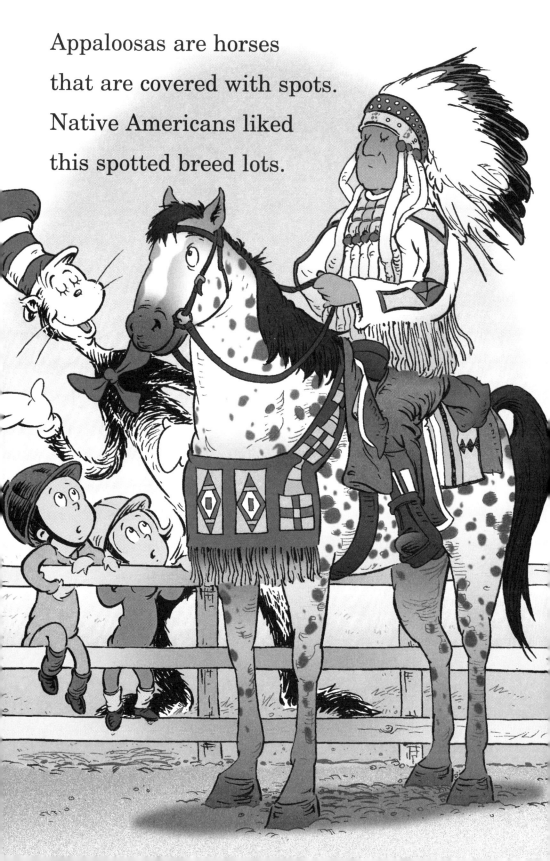

In the sandy Sahara
the Arabian's a prize.
It has grace and speed
and a delicate size.

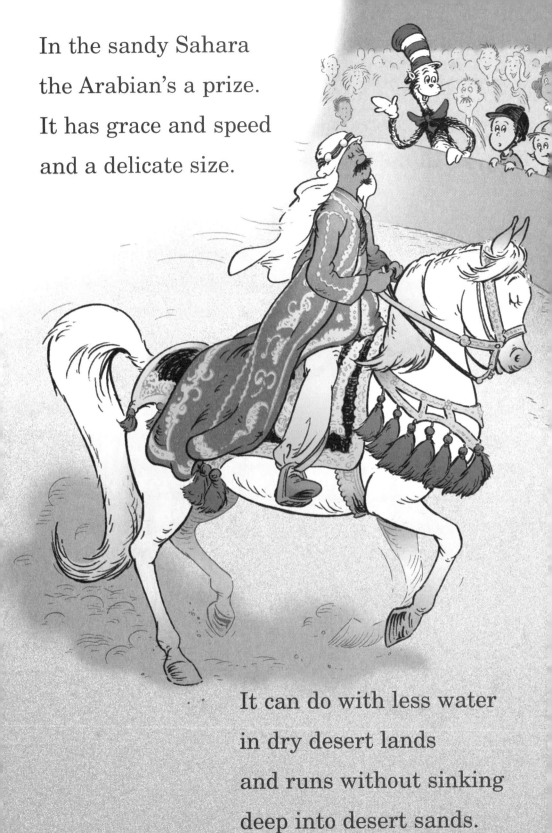

It can do with less water
in dry desert lands
and runs without sinking
deep into desert sands.

Arabians now live
the whole world round.
Where there are horse lovers,
this breed can be found.

With large eyes and nostrils
and a dainty muzzle,
it's easy to handle
and happy to nuzzle.

The Fjord (FEE-ord), from Norway,
can deal with rough weather.
They say it is stronger
than good, tough shoe leather.

Australian stock horses—
sometimes called Walers—
came Down Under with British
settlers and sailors.

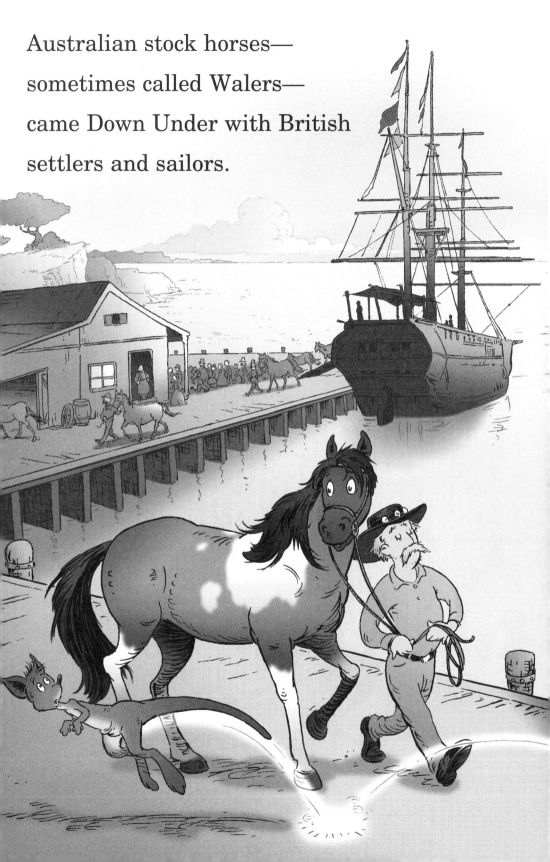

Connemara ponies go
on great riding tours
of Ireland's fair marshes
and its rolling moors.

These hunters and jumpers—
so the story goes—
swam from Spanish shipwrecks.
But who really knows!

Answer this question
and you'll win a prize.
Is being a pony
a matter of size?

A grown horse that's less
than fourteen hands, two
you say is a pony.
The prize goes to you!

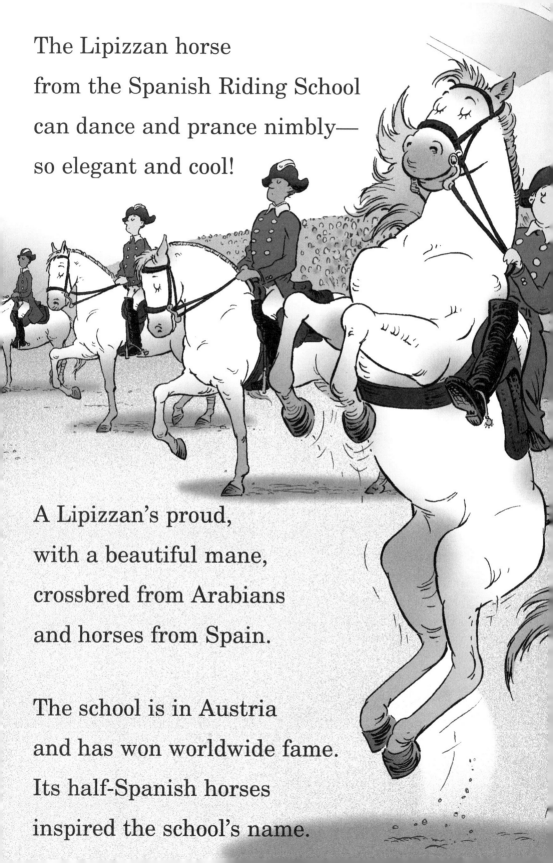

The Lipizzan horse
from the Spanish Riding School
can dance and prance nimbly—
so elegant and cool!

A Lipizzan's proud,
with a beautiful mane,
crossbred from Arabians
and horses from Spain.

The school is in Austria
and has won worldwide fame.
Its half-Spanish horses
inspired the school's name.

The Morgan is smart
and learns quickly how
to pull rigs, plow the fields,
run a race, herd a cow.

Thoroughbred is a horse
born and bred for the track.
It carries a jockey
upon its sleek back.

It runs in big races
of worldwide renown
like the Ascot, the Epsom
and the Triple Crown.

Mustangs roam wild
on the wide-open plains.
They've never known saddles
or the feel of the reins.

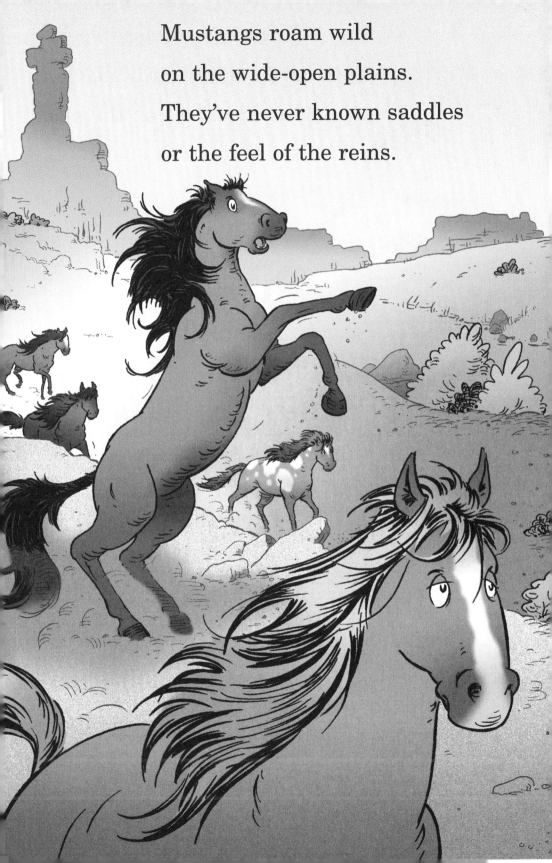

Bit, reins, and saddle
are what we call tack.
Reins and bit on the head,
saddle over the back.

BIT

HEADSTALL

CANTLE

HORN

POMMEL

JOCKEY

CHIN
STRAP

SEAT

REAR
JOCKE

GULLET

REINS

LATIGO
KEEPER

LATIGO

SKIRT

CINCH
RING

STIRRUP
LEATHER

STIRRUP

CINCH

WESTERN

here are western saddles
nd the English kind.
he difference between them
t us bear in mind.

BROWBAND

HEADSTALL

CHEEK
PIECE

NOSEBAND

THROATLATCH

CANTLE

POMMEL

REINS

GULLET

SEAT

BIT

FLAP

GIRTH

LEATHERS

STIRRUP
IRON

ENGLISH

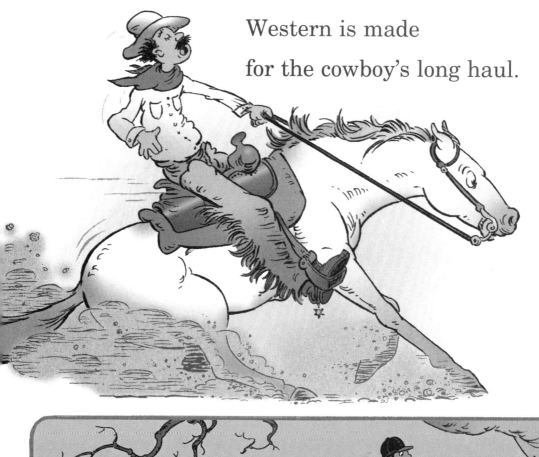

Western is made
for the cowboy's long haul.

English is for hunting and
jumping and all.

On English, we post
and we must learn the knack
of rising up off of
the trotting horse back.

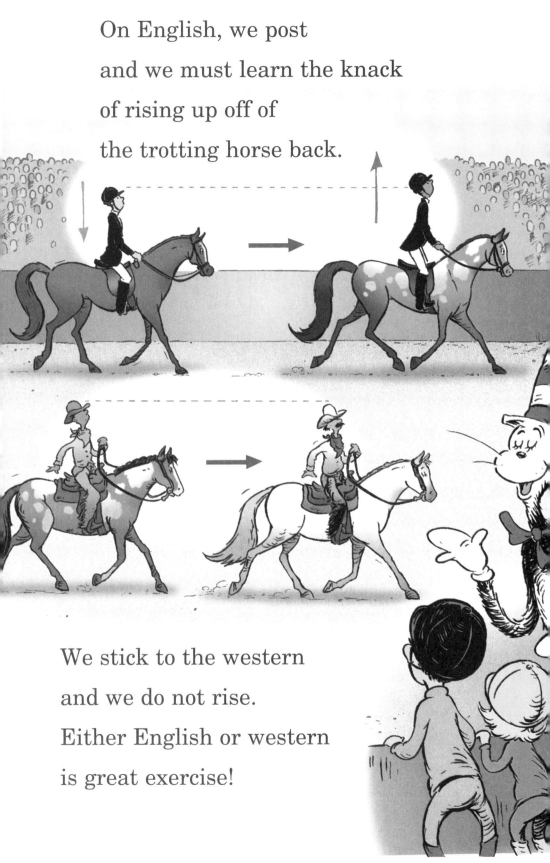

We stick to the western
and we do not rise.
Either English or western
is great exercise!

Now put on the saddle,
the reins, and the bit.
Your hard riding cap—
you can't forget it!

The judges are waiting.
It's time for the show.
So pick up the reins . . .

. . . giddyup and let's go!

GLOSSARY

Down Under: A term used for Australia, which is "down under" the equator.

Farrier: A person trained to put shoes on horses.

Hie: To go quickly.

Inspired: Filled with the spirit to do something.

Jockey: A person who rides a racehorse.

Knack: A special ability.

Moor: Grassy, wind-swept land with few trees.

Nary a: Another way of saying "not one."

Nimbly: Lightly and quickly.

Post: To rise and fall with the movement of a trotting horse.

Predator: A hunter.

Prey: An animal that is hunted.

Trait: An inherited quality.

FOR FURTHER READING

The Girl Who Loved Wild Horses by Paul Goble (Richard Jackson Books). A Caldecott Award–winning folktale about a Native American girl's love of horses. For ages 4–8.

Horse by Juliet Clutton-Brock (DK Publishing, *DK Eyewitness Books*). All about horses—their history, anatomy, and breeds and the many different jobs they do. For grades 3 and up.

Horse Heroes: True Stories of Amazing Horses by Kate Petty (DK Publishing, *DK Readers*, Level 4). Famous horses throughout history. For grades 3–5.

A Horse Named Seabiscuit by Cathy East Dubowski and Mark Dubowski, illustrated by Michael Langham Rowe (Grosset & Dunlap, *All Aboard Reading*, Station Stop 3). The true story of an unlikely champion. For ages 4–8.

Horse Song: The Naadam of Mongolia by Ted and Betsy Lewin (Lee & Low Books). The story of a young boy who rides his horse for the first time in Naadam, the Mongolian summer festival. For grades 2–5.

Judy Richter's Riding for Kids (Storey Publishing). An introduction to horsemanship by a highly regarded instructor. For ages 9–12.

INDEX